BRAIN
Beauty

THE ULTIMATE MAKEUP GUIDE
FOR YOUR
MIND, BODY AND SOUL

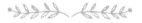

CELEBRITY MAKEUP ARTIST
DR. KYM LEE KING

Copyright ©2019 Dr. Kym Lee King

Published by
Live Limitless Authors Academy & Publishing Co.
Publishing@sierrarainge.com

Dr. Kym Lee King Contact Information :
Email: winknpout1@gmail.com
Website: www.winknpoutbykymlee.com

Printed in the United States of America
Cover Design by: Adam I. Wade
Cover Photo by: Jackie Hicks of Fond Memories Photography

ISBN: 978-1-7340469-5-3

Library of Congress Number: 2019915499

Dedication

This book is dedicated to women all around the world who have experienced a broken heart, shattered self-esteem and diminished self-worth. I wrote this book as a guide and daily reminder that you are enough, your beauty is insurmountable and you are not alone.

Brain Beauty

Acknowledgements

I'd like to first and foremost acknowledge God who is the center and source of all of my gifts, desires and success. Jesus has been a constant force and a very present HELP. To my husband, who is my biggest fan and greatest supporter, thank you for all of your unwavering and unconditional love that has continued to lift me from doubt and small thinking. Thank you for standing strongly by my side during moments of weakness and for leading our family in love and legacy. Your laughter and witty sense of humor brings me so much joy each day. You are my best friend, my confidant and my lifetime love. I love you forever, always and in ALL ways.

To our beautiful children and collectively we have quite a few, Nicholas, Ronaz, Byron, Elijah, Taylor, Symone, My Love children, Nathan, Darian, Joseph, William, Ryan, Rashaad, Ronald, J'Nya and to my grandson Nasir for allowing me to love unconditionally.

Writing a book is harder than I thought and more rewarding than I could have ever imagined. None of this would have been possible without my loving parents Edgar and Sheila Gay for exposing me to a life that pointed me in the direction of greatness. They taught me discipline, unconditional love, manners, etiquette, respect, and so much more that has helped me to soar in life.

To my mother Bunny, my sister Jennifer, and the Alston family. God's grace and favor was extended by reuniting me with my family.

To my brothers Manny, Ronald, James, Gerald, and, Miztah Charles blood could not make us any closer... your love, protection, laughter, and continued support are most appreciated.

As I sit and ponder on the sincerest elation of being able to author my first book, I am compelled to express my most genuine appreciation for the many who have assisted me through this process with love, support, encouragement and prayer.

I wish to extend profound affection to my dearest friends and sisters, Kimberly, Lolita, Yvonne, Sherritta, Stephanie, Raquel, Deya, LaTonya H, Tonya K, Dionna,

Acknowledgements

Cheryl J, Sharnetta, Precious, Wendy, Dionne, Bridget, Janeise, Janette, Lachelle, Dawn, Charese, Dee-Dee, Mercedes, Sheryl, Joyce, Debbie, Tam, Germaine, Letitia, Jackie, Brely, Angelique, and "The CCC's," for your unwavering love and belief in my potential. You all inspire me at my absolute best at everything that I do is because I know that you guys expect nothing less than greatness from me. Your support fuels me and I love you all dearly.

I would like to express my sincere gratitude to my mentors for being exactly what I needed, and exactly when I needed it. Your honesty and candor always helps to keep me on track.

To my mentors and confidants:

Dr. Medina Pullings & Pastor Orrin Pullings

Dr. Vikki Johnson

Elder Sherri Griffin & Donnell Griffin

Vanessa Banks

Derrick Rutledge, Makeup Maestro

Harvey Star Washington

Coleen Otero, and the CEO Chicks

Marietta Carter-Narcisse

THANK YOU for your listening ears and wise words of counsel, guidance, love and truth.

I would like to pay tribute to my publisher Sierra Rainge-Jones and the team at Live Limitless Author's Academy for your support and collaboration, without you, birthing this book would not have been possible

To my Forward church family and "Tribe" your love is steadfast and warmly appreciated. Your continued support for my projects and dreams have made my heart smile each day. Thank you for loving me as your first lady and Co-Pastor.

To my God parents Pastors James & Pamela Sturdivant, (and FUM Family) my admiration for you is beyond words ... thank you for ALWAYS covering me!

To the first lady's and Co-pastors who have wholeheartedly made an impact in my life, Nakia Wright, Rochelle Wilson, Weptomah Davis, Faye Bell, Wendy Nelson, Aisha Staples, Phaedra Johnson, Anita Phillips, Shelby Teague, Chrystal White, Jacqueline Duncan You are the ultimate example of strength and integrity who are in ministry holding up the arms of your amazing husbands ... thank you for being a constant example of excellence!

Acknowledgements

Thank you to the pastors and senior statesman who have helped to shape my spiritual life and walk, Bishop T.D. Jakes and Lady Serita Jakes, Bishop Glen A Staples, Bishop Alfred and Co-Pastor Susie Owens, Bishop Joel Peebles and Ylawnda Peebles, Bishop John and Co-Pastor Ernestine Lewis, Drs. Mike and Dee-Dee Freeman, Pastors Grainger and Co-Pastor Joan Browning, Fondrea Lewis, Jamal Bryant, Bishop Robert Perry.

To my Prayer Partners

Angela Thornton, Linda Evans, Gloria Boone, Karon Yarborough, Wendy Trice, The women of Empowerment & Destiny and the Forward church 6am morning prayer call intercessors

My GLAM FAM ...

Vernon, Quentin, Ishia, China, Evie, Jamal, Keith Harley, Goo-Goo, Barry Fletcher, Vanessa Flemming, Andrea Cheese, Angie Mac, Randy, Deandre, Jenn, Danessa, Debbie Johnson, Tameka Butler, Letitia Thornhill, Germaine Williams, Maggy Franscois, The WinknPout Academy... And to every MUA, Hairstylist, Wardrobe Stylist, Barber, nail tech, photographer, videographer, lighting Tech, producer, director, writer ... I've ever been blessed to work with, I take a piece of you with me wherever I go. Your passion, and creative gifts are priceless... together we create magic each day that the world dreams about. We are the essence of beauty. Thank you for sharing your talents with me.

#PrettyKymittee for your years of support! Thank you for rocking with me on social media. You are my cyber gangsters.

Writing a book about the story of my life is a surreal process. I'm forever indebted to you all.

Thank you to women of Distinction in my glorious sorority of Delta Sigma Theta! Let's continue to trail-blaze and shine, the world is watching as we lead by example.

Special THANKS and gratitude to my managers Vern Golf and Adean King

You both have believed in me, rallied for me and pushed me beyond words. Your dedication and support does not go unnoticed. You are my Rocks!

A special thank you To Jamie Foster Brown & Raymone Bain for always exposing me to a world of glamour and dreams. As a young woman and artist I lived vicariously through your life of splendor.

And to my colleagues... specifically Jawn Murray for always allowing me to sound off my ideas, dreams and aspirations! You have helped to propel my visions to flight. Thank you!

Thank you Black Entertainment Television for allowing me to paint beautiful faces over your airwaves for over 22 years. It was never work but I always felt like I was "Living the Dream".

Thank you Debra Lee for allowing me to be a part of your A-Team for 15+ years. My heart is forever grateful to you.

To all of the aforementioned people and to those I neglected to mention thank you, THANK YOU, THANK YOU!!

Brain Beauty

FOREWORD

*From Golden Globe
Award Winning Actress and Activist*
Angela Bassett

Bravo to Dr. Kym Lee-King for taking the steps to discover Brain Beauty. For over ten years, I have witnessed her passion and dedication to women as she has provided me with glamour services on countless movie sets, award shows, events and television productions. She is truly an expert on beauty acquisition and transformation. I am thrilled that she is sharing her heart and wisdom in book form. She has been my trusted friend, sister, and a part of my Glam squad for many years and I'm confident that the 10 beauty commandments in this book will help you live a life that is both divine and destined.

When I think of beauty, I can't help but reflect on my journey of discovering my purpose.

I'm often asked in interviews if my portrayal of smart and strong women in my career has been on purpose. The word purpose and what it means has filled my spirit. The truth is that we all have a purpose, even if we are still striving to understand what it is. When I decided as a teenager that acting would be my path, whether I recognized it or not, I was walking towards my purpose. As a young actress trying to make my way, survival figured into the equation, but not so much that I was ever willing to compromise my integrity.

The path hasn't always been easy, and there have been tough times and days when the phone didn't ring; Even after "What's Love Got to Do With It", as well as moments of uncertainty and doubt. But, what women like my mother Betty Jane and my aunt Golden taught me, is that there will be times when you seemingly face insurmountable obstacles, but that's when you dig deep into your soul for the courage and the fortitude to keep going, and to never forget that despite life's detours you are destined for greatness.

It's so important that we have access to books like "Brain Beauty" that help us expand our vision, even when we sometimes lose sight of it due to the distractions of life's many challenges.

Foreword

As you're reading this book, show gratitude for those who inspire your growth because none of us arrive by ourselves. We are shaped, molded and fueled by the support of powerful women around us. It's this sense of community that feeds our souls when we're running on empty.

So, when you're told that you're not good enough, you tell them, not only am I Good enough.... I'm MORE than enough!

When people tell you that you're mean or nasty for having boundaries ... you tell them ... this is me and I am resolute ... and I'm standing in my truth!

And when they say you're not beautiful... you tell them you are the descendant of royalty. You are a queen!

We have much work to do but together we are unstoppable!

It's time to find your purpose and pursue it passionately, purposefully and loudly! It's time for women to heal and grow, to be persistent and win!

Understand, that in order to win in the world, you must first win within. So, take care of your mind, nurture your soul and exercise your body. You are capable of doing great things, but your first role; your first assignment is yourself. Show up as the most beautiful version of who you are, bring your beauty with you everywhere you go. When you walk into a room command the space with your confidence, grace and presence. Be less critical of yourself and others and always honor the star within. You are worth it, you deserve it and it's your birthright. This book has been designed to help you discover, honor, celebrate, love and work on yourself. So enjoy the journey to Ultimate Brain Beauty.

With Love,

Angela Bassett

Brain Beauty Open Letter

Welcome to Brain Beauty ... My objective as a beauty professional and confidence coach is to accentuate beauty physically, but also to insightfully encourage beauty psychologically.

Your body is your sacred temple, it houses your mind, intellect, feelings, thoughts, dreams and visions.

Have you ever looked in the mirror and dreaded the reflection looking back at you? Have you ever scrolled through your timeline and all of a sudden felt depressed? Inadequate? Ugly? Have you ever compromised your integrity or settled for less than what you truly deserved only because you didn't feel as though you deserved more?

Your whole body, as well as your entire sense of being must submit to a wellness regimen in order to operate at the most optimal capacity. The truth is, you cannot draw from an empty well, so maintaining your well-being is critical to your ability to operate at your greatest potential.

Often times, women are consumed with caring for and tending to everything around them while subsequently putting off or neglecting their own needs.

It's imperative that we prioritize rest so that we can get replenished adequately. You'd be amazed at just how efficiently a well-rested mind and body functions. When provided with the appropriate amount of rest, rejuvenation, reflection and restoration, we are then fortified in our personal esteem and overall sense of wellness.

You may be wondering how I gained such a love for and interest in both inner and outer beauty transformation along with its profound effects on self-esteem;

I realized many years ago that my passion met my purpose while working with some of the most noted celebrities in the world. These women were highly celebrated around the globe, yet they weren't able to escape feelings of discouragement and hurt that accompany the human experience. When these women sat in my chair, I found that as I was curating a custom look for them on the outside, our conversations and connectedness was stirring a transformation on the inside; One that would radiate outwardly and display the true essence of beauty.

These were women who had it all. They were successful singers, acclaimed actors, and business moguls with thriving bank accounts.

You would think that instant beauty was at their fingertips and could be purchased so easily on demand.

Having access to the best plastic surgeons allowed nip and tuck procedures to be just a phone call away. The truth of the matter is that any beauty enhancement could be purchased with ease.

But, I too had a self-discovery moment, and one that would change the course of my life forever. It had nothing to do with a physical change from surgery. To be quite honest, this secret I lived with is the primary purpose for me writing this book. I can remember the day I received the phone call from a state agency that I had someone "Looking for me." And that person being my mother. Yes, MY MOTHER! At 35 years old, I was introduced to my biological mother after having no idea that I was ever adopted. My emotions were raging with unanswered questions, of WHY? My mind was consumed and even overwhelmed with wonder, all while the enemy attempted to plague my mind with overwhelming thoughts of rejection and discouragement. Even after years of accomplishments, graduations, giving birth to my son, and traveling the world; this discovery made me feel like I was robbed of the fullness of my identity. In my mind, I felt betrayed. I wrestled with this lie for years. Yes, I was still "Kym Lee" to the public, but the state had me documented by a different birth name to a set of parents I never knew. Imagine discovering this at one of the best times of your life. Life often throws us curve balls that jilt our esteem, like divorce, infidelity, sickness, and financial struggles. But there is always hope.

There are some of you reading this that may have similar experiences. You too may have struggled with an identity crisis; and if we're speaking honestly, some of you still haven't recovered. Today all of that changes. ***Brain Beauty*** will be the ultimate guide to help you re-paint your mind body and soul, while learning to forgive, and discover who you really are.

No matter what our status in life is, there in an internal clean up required to experience happiness, confidence and an enhanced sense of self. While we are able to paint our faces, not even our best foundation brushes can stroke the scars that blemish the soul. Ultimately, although our stories read differently the only thing separating me from you or my clients is a cape. Not just the figurative cape that women so often wear as we take on the world, but the protective barrier between the women being serviced and myself. More importantly our hearts are knitted with the same issues, similar pain points, battles with low self-esteem, un-forgiveness and more.

Throughout the years, we've been inundated with women's empowerment events, seminars and movements stemming around self-esteem and personal development. So often we show up to events but for some reason, many of us ignore the steps that lead to self-worth. This is usually because we don't truly believe that we are worthy. We forget that beauty must be established from within. Only then will we rise above the need for outward validation. When we love ourselves first, we set the standard. Your worth is not measured by the number of likes you receive on a post, or the amount of comments garnered from sharing your highlight reel on your social site of choice.

Many of the people we yearn to receive social approval from are carefully curating online content that is a fabricated exaggeration of who they want others to believe they are. Cyber validation is in fact, a false pretense of thoughts gathered from people who aren't really who they claim to be in the first place.

Unfortunately we have given these very same people permission to validate us. The danger in this is that if you live from the applause of others you will be crushed by their criticism as well.

When we give others so much power over us, it causes us to operate as a caricature of who others expect us to be. This is why the world has mastered the art of masking their pain but fail epically at showing up authentically.

Unfortunately, this trend has led many to establish self-sabotaging habits. This destructive trait is to blame for countless sleepless nights that individuals spend scrolling and comparing their real lives to someone else's carefully staged and edited photos. Comparison steals joy, sabotages confidence and has unfortunately even led some to suicide.

So, you mean to tell me that we have arbitrarily given our esteem away to strangers who probably don't think as highly of themselves as they claim or project online? The answer is YES!

If you are guilty of placing a portion of yourself that is so precious, into the hands of a stranger or a loved one who abuses your heart with negative words, then today we are on a mission to regain those misplaced emotions! We must always keep in mind that anyone who doesn't inspire our growth or reciprocate our support must never have open access to our hearts. That also includes colleagues or clients who don't honor our value.

You see, I spent many years silently searching for others to make me feel good about myself, and my work. So, I know first-hand how heavy it is to crave approval and to carry the burden of criticism from others. Most artists are recognized and feel validated based off of the approval of others. Perhaps you picked up this book because you too are tired of these wavering opinions. Or maybe you're tired of adorning yourself on the outside, while still suffering with self-esteem deficiencies on the inside.

Well, I have GREAT news, I want you to know is that your self-esteem belongs to you and today you're snatching it back!

I wrote this book as a makeup guide to help you discover and own your full beauty. This book is a tool to help you honor the true essence of your mind, body and soul.

Self-esteem is made up of the thoughts, feelings, and opinions we have about ourselves, coupled with the thoughts and feelings that others have about us.

The operative word is "SELF", so that means it belongs to you and it is your responsibility to develop and nurture it. As you read, I will be enforcing the importance of self-care and why it's NOT selfish, but rather a significant component of self-preservation.

As you turn the pages, I will engage your thoughts while encouraging you to consider your own needs more by guarding yourself from the negative opinions of outside influences.

I mean, would you allow a thief into your home and run the risk of them taking something valuable? You would most likely refuse them entry.

So why then, would you allow the opinions of others to invade your thoughts and beliefs, robbing you of the invaluable jewels that reside in your esteem?

Self-esteem for many of us is a work in progress that we must tend to often. The way we perceive ourselves isn't fixed, it has the propensity to change, depending on the way we think. Over time, habits of negative thinking and destructive self-talk can become a severe detriment to the way we see and value ourselves.

My heart's desire is for women to get to a point where their sense of identity isn't completely wrapped up in how other's perceive them. We must obtain our sense of identity from something stable. Something that is unchanging.

There will always be more ways to make yourself outwardly beautiful, and there will always be more ways to work on yourself in order to achieve inward beauty.

So how do we become more inwardly beautiful? It begins with pure thoughts and it is based on the word of GOD.

While we equate beauty to physical appearance or happiness, God equates beauty to holiness. "O worship the LORD in the beauty of holiness: fear before him, all the earth." – *Psalm 96:9*

The biggest inhibitor to the beauty of holiness is the ugliness of sin.

God can take your ugly insides and make them drop dead gorgeous. He wants to! It's His desire to bless us. He can heal the wounds that we are ashamed of and turn them into beautiful scars. As Isaiah 61:3 puts it, *"...to give unto them beauty for ashes..."*

2 Corinthians 3:18 says, *"But we all, with unveiled face beholding as in a mirror the glory of the Lord, are changed into the same image from glory to glory, even as by the Spirit of the Lord."*

We can always become more inwardly beautiful because we can always become more holy. From glory to glory... more and more. 1 Peter 1:15 instructs us, *"But just as he who called you is holy, so be holy in all you do..."*

I want to take you back to a moment where I hit a brick wall and I felt that my world was falling apart, All that I had worked for and accomplished carried no weight because I did not love myself.

I eventually arrived at the understanding that self-love was missing when I found myself in a series of failed relationships. My love life was like a drama filled reality show, full of deceit, lies, cheating and a few instances of abuse. During that period in my life, I was making great business decisions but very bad personal decisions. I was winning in public and suffering in private. My personal life looked nothing like my professional life. I hate to admit this, but my personal life was in shambles. It was full of low moments. I would have highs of working with celebrities, going to award shows, being featured in magazines, attending the Grammys and Essence festival, only to return home to a life that was much less than what I deserved.

The way I neglected my body caused consequent weight gain. I wasn't working out or eating right because I was trying to keep up with the fast paced work life that I had created. I scheduled and prioritized clients but neglected myself. I let broken people (men I dated) to take ownership over my heart and mind, when they themselves weren't whole or healed. Covering my insecurities was never their responsibility and they weren't equipped to fill the void that I needed.

One day, as I was sitting with my thoughts, I said to myself, "Here I am empty" and because I was not whole, I was attracting people who were just like me. I was looking for outside love to fill my voids, and then experiencing disappointment when I realized that they didn't have the capacity to fill me. I needed to declutter my heart, my mind and my soul.

Are you allowing wrong decisions and inconsistent relationships to clog your pores? What's causing you not to breathe and grow? Everyday your skin is growing, so a dead layer of skin must be removed daily in order to reveal the good skin beneath the surface. So certainly we must unclog our emotional pores to ensure growth in our hearts and in our minds. If you will agree to implement these tools, I can guarantee that your mind will be free and your heart will be ready to receive the abundance of love that you deserve.

"Those who look to him are radiant, and their faces shall never be ashamed." – Psalms 34:5

Introduction

As a celebrity makeup artist, I've been blessed with so many amazing opportunities to travel the globe and work with some of the world's most talented and glamorous stars. I've had the honor of being able to share, speak, and teach at countless women's conferences, churches, retreats and empowerment events. What I've discovered about women, is that we all have a desire to feel beautiful, to be accepted, to be loved, and to shine in our personal star power.

There's a sense of fulfillment that I experience when I use my skills and love for makeup art to enhance a woman's beauty. I'm always fascinated that with a few strokes of my brush, a vision for beauty, some attention to detail and a love for all things couture, I'm able to paint a version of pretty that compels a sense of confidence and self-acceptance.

It's funny how concealing, contouring and highlighting the right parts of a woman's face instantly reveals an enhanced version of her expression. We adorn ourselves with jewels, lip stick, eyelashes and blush to feel put together, to feel pretty enough; as if the way we look is the ultimate qualifier for self-worth.

While I truly enjoy creating an outward enhancement, it's the inner transformation that is most profound. If we're not careful, we will invest time, energy and focus on perfecting our look while neglecting our emotional, mental and spiritual maintenance. This results in looking pretty but lacking purpose or even worse, appearing beautiful while secretly suffering with inner brokenness.

Women tend to focus more on fixing their outer reflection because it's typically a quick fix. However, while the results are instant, they are only temporary.

When you wash your face, and wipe away your Maybeline, Fenty, Lancome, M.A.C or your exclusive Wink & Pout products, does your confidence and self -love roll down the sink and into the drain along with your mascara and foundation residue?

Do you retain your boldness and sense of beauty? Have you worked on the blemished parts of your character? Or have you settled for the shallow satisfaction of just looking the part?

I remember when my husband and I were dating. Before he would come over, I would prepare for him by making sure that I looked good. I would be sure to beat my face, put on my most flattering outfits, make sure my home was clean and the air was freshened with my favorite scent of Febreze. I always wanted to look good for my man. It wasn't until he showed up to visit me one evening before I could fix my hair and beat my face that I realized that the part of me that needed the most "makeup" was my mind and my soul. When he walked in, I ran to hide and cover myself up. I remember falling in love deeper with my husband that day. When he saw me in raw form, and he assured me of his lasting and unconditional love for me. He told me I was beautiful and that he loved me with or without any artificial additions. In that moment, I was so relieved that I no longer had to hide myself, but I was alarmed that I had held on to the fear of true authenticity for too long.

What I know for sure is that there are some parts of who you are that you can't filter or Photoshop. There is no app that can instantly remove, fear, doubt, insecurity, low self-esteem or feelings of inadequacy. These imperfections are not resolved with photo finish foundation. These are the pieces of us that require soul searching, self-assessment and soul work.

This book is the ultimate beauty guide for your mind, body and soul. Through daily devotions, personal stories, and insight into the life lessons that have been shaped by personal, professional, and spiritual development, I walk you through the 10 commandments of true beauty by implementing the makeup process to look good and live your best life from the inside out.

This is makeup for your mind. This is BRAIN BEAUTY.

While reading this book, get ready for a life-changing makeover, turn the pages and take the journey with me.

Table of Contents

COMMANDMENT 1

Shelf Life

"Thou shall NOT allow anything ugly
from my past to prevent me from my
beautiful future"

What is Shelf-life ?

Pro Tip:

The aim of shelf-life is to help consumers make safe and informed use of products and/or food. The shelf-life of these should only be considered valid, if the product is purchased intact and undamaged. Consumers should always follow manufacturers' instructions on storage, particularly temperature and use of the product after opening.

It is imperative that you know how to recognize when something is outdated from both a product and spiritual perspective.

makeup
EXPIRATION CHART
BY KYM LEE-KING

LIQUIDS & CREAMS

PRIMER	
FOUNDATION	6-12 M
CONCEALER	6-12 M
CONTOUR/BRONZER	6-12 M
BLUSH	1 Y
HIGHLIGHTER	6-12 M
BROW GEL	6-12 M
BROW POMADE	6 M
SETTING SPRAY	6 M
	1-2 Y

LIPS

BULLET LIPSTICK	2 Y
LIQUID LIPSTICK	1-2 Y
LIP GLOSS	1 Y
LIP LINER	2 Y

POWDERS

PRESSED FOUNDATION	2-3 Y
LOOSE POWDER	1-2 Y
CONTOUR/BRONZER	1-2 Y
BLUSH	1-2 Y
HIGHLIGHTER	1-2 Y
BROW POWDER	1-2 Y

EYES

MASCARA	3-6 M
LIQUID EYELINER	6 M
GEL EYELINER	6 M
PENCIL EYELINERS	1-2 Y
EYESHADOW	6 M - 3 Y
LIQUID EYESHADOW	6-12 M

WHILE THIS CHART PROVIDES A GUIDELINE TO EXPIRATION DATES,
ALWAYS CHECK YOUR PERSONAL PRODUCTS FOR A PRODUCT AFTER
OPENING (PAO) SYMBOL. THE PAO WILL INCLUDE THE NUMBER OF
MONTHS THAT SPECIFIC PRODUCT IS GOOD FOR AFTER YOU OPEN IT.
FOLLOW THE PAO SYMBOL INSTEAD OF THIS CHART IF THEY DIFFER.

On the back of most beauty products you will find these characters that indicate how long a product will last after opening the package. Conduct inventory, and then toss out the outdated products so that you can prepare for and create space for new inventory.

Welcome to the last day of your past! Get a quick glimpse of those heartbreaks and disappoints, those hard to forget moments of internal frustration, and tell them ALL Goodbye! Our past can never be changed and if we're learning from our lessons, mistakes from our past should not be repeated. But, for some reason, we like to dance with thoughts, frustrations and missteps that we've forged in our history. Typically, those thoughts are filled with moments of regret and sorrow from experiences that we are unable to retract.

I like to metaphorically think of my past as expired milk or old food where the shelf life has long run out. What was once good for us can now make us sick when consumed after the appointed dates. When things go bad, we don't usually consume them. For the most part, we assume that if we did, we would get sick!

You should treat your past in the same manner. Anything that has expired should not be consumed! For instance, if a relationship is over, release it so that the weight of its absence does not anchor you in disappointment. If a friendship has arrived at its point of departure, understand that you are the CEO of your life, which means that you can choose when to walk away from people who you may have outgrown. Remember, old habits, bad relationships, and negative thoughts are the core of low-esteem and should always be treated as invalid.

We have given people the keys to our esteem and allowed them to govern our thoughts long enough. Like a thief in the night, their words and actions have robbed us of the precious commodity that is self-love.

It is our responsibility to reclaim our love and regard for ourselves so that we can also gain the wisdom, strength and fortitude to manage and master our emotions. Remember, the operative word in SELF-esteem is SELF. It belongs to YOU!

When we begin to consider products that work to give us a desired effect, we have to first think about if the product works for the purpose in which it was created for. Shelf life in the beauty industry refers to the length of time for which a product remains usable, fit for consumption, or saleable.

Even in the most eye catching packaging on the shelf, when the product has exceeded its shelf life, it's efficacy has diminished.

It makes no sense to purchase and utilize a product, when the purpose for which you purchased it can no longer be guaranteed. So, even with the best branding and a seal still intact, the product is of no value.

Are there things in your life that have expired, yet you are keeping them on the shelf? Are you using outdated methods? Engaging in outdated relationships? What are the things in your life that have exceeded their shelf life but are still taking up space?

Old words? Old habits? Old excuses? Past experiences? We need to give all of our ex's a pink slip. Ex-boyfriends, Ex-bosses, Ex-friends, Ex-addictions, etc. We have employed and allowed them to rule our world for long enough. Their time has expired! It's like eating old food, it will make you sick.

Assess the things in your life that are alive and decide which are dead. When you come to the understanding that the shelf life is done, there is no reason to continue in consumption; especially when you're not getting desirable results?

Let go of anything that does not line up with what is growing in your life.

Just because you may have been convicted of a crime, struggled with an addiction, made some mistakes, had an abortion, or went bankrupt; Know that all of these situations are products of your past, and you do not have to allow them to dictate your future. These are old habits, old beliefs, and ultimately old aspects are who you used to be. Your past mistakes are no longer valid and can only limit you if you choose to allow them to.

The truth is, a lot of the things that we are holding onto are outdated. I encourage you to let go of the weight of everything in your life that needs to be discontinued.

It will require daily effort and proactive living. You must learn to be less reactive so that you can get ahead of resistance.

 **STAR MOMENT**

Fantasia Barrino-Taylor

There are moments when adversity silences us and our gifts remain dormant. From past mistakes to rumors and guilt, the enemy is an accuser of Gods beloved; but this song bird never allowed her adversity to take her voice. I was blessed to travel the world with Fantasia during some of her life's most difficult moments. I witnessed her discard the "expired" feelings and one of the most resilient voices to grace the earth is Fantasia. The ability to discard what we used to hold in high regard, is one of the most challenging things to do. To throw away what we thought we could not live without is difficult for most but I remember fantasia doing just that during my time working with her. I've seen her discard the old and replace it with the new. I would call her the "come-back kid." The remarkable ability to overcome illiteracy, being a single mom, failed relationships, and even a struggling career. I've seen her wipe it off, realize that when a period is over and then move on to what was better.

My moments with Fantasia were very endearing and meaningful. Every encounter with her was always humbling. We grew up in the same church organization with similar beliefs in God, family, friendships, motherhood, etc. Most of our glam sessions were filled with laughter, love and even worship in some moments. We were two church girls who beat the odds. In spite of our past mistakes and regardless of what was ever rumored about our decisions, we made it by the grace of GOD! We were adamant about implementing the lessons that we had learned that helped us to release any part of our ugly past. We recognized that releasing it was the solution to our beautiful future! Fantasia is my hero and one of the greatest examples of Gods redemption. Before marrying my husband we were at one of her tour stops and I remember her saying to me so vividly. "Cherish every moment with your KING ... God gave you another chance at LOVE".

DEVOTIONAL PRAYER
FOR YOUR MAKEUP KIT

"Lord help me to forgive those who have hurt me because I cannot change what happened in my past. In like manner, help me to forgive myself for entertaining sabotaging thoughts. Help me to extend myself grace in spite of my previous mistakes and poor choices. Help me to NOT allow the words or opinions of others to stop me from activating and operating in my purpose. When the words of my peers and counterparts fail to line up with your plans for my life, please erase them from my memory in Jesus' name, Amen!"

Notes and Reflections

Soul Work

To Do List:

_____ ☐
_____ ☐
_____ ☐
_____ ☐
_____ ☐
_____ ☐
_____ ☐
_____ ☐
_____ ☐

Goals

_____
_____
_____
_____
_____
_____
_____
_____
_____

Today's Devotion

_____
_____
_____
_____
_____
_____
_____
_____
_____
_____

Personal Affirmations

_____
_____
_____
_____
_____
_____
_____
_____
_____
_____

Reflections

_____

_____

_____

_____

_____

_____

_____

_____

_____

_____

_____

_____

_____

_____

_____

_____

_____

_____

_____

_____

_____

_____

_____

_____

_____

COMMANDMENT 2

Cleansing /Exfoliating
The Strip down

"Thou shall cleanse thy mind,
body and soul DAILY"

This is a chapter on forgiveness and removal. Commandment 2 is a call to action to employ once you've mastered the importance of letting go of expired things in your life. It's the daily work needed to maintain a flawless mind.

It is imperative that you recognize when something is outdated from both a product perspective, and a spiritual lens.

Pro Tip

A cleanser is a facial care product that is used to remove makeup, dead skin cells, oil, dirt, and other types of pollutants from the skin of the face.

PRODUCT PERSPECTIVE

Physical cleansers allow you to go deep. The type of strip down depends on the surface that it is working to clean. The type of product I choose to use on a client depends on the problem that is present. If someone has sensitive skin, then I wouldn't suggest using a product that is likely to irritate the skin.

SPIRITUAL LENS

From the outlook of faith, your spiritual lens allows you to discern issues while giving you insight on the necessary action steps to help you generate resolve. It's when you recognize the issue and you proceed with employing the work required. This can include counseling, therapy, rehab, forgiveness, and even no longer being bitter.

We tend to cover our issues with being busy. Placing demands on our time is the makeup that we wear to conceal our inability to simply be still and deal with conflict. The question we must ask ourselves is, "what will work to clear up the issue at hand?" For instance, a person with large pores is more susceptible to bacteria which makes them more likely to get acne.

Just like a person with a large heart tends to get hurt more. When your heart is open but not guarded, you are vulnerable to toxicity. The problems that we experience often vary. This is why you can't always use the same skincare products that your friends use. Their regimen may not be effective for you if you don't have the same skin condition.

Often times, we are misdiagnosed when in reality our issues aren't that deep.

Your problem may not be as big as you think they are. If you overstimulate the pores; it will produce more oil than needed and create problems that weren't there before.

When you're feeling completely overwhelmed with emotions, it's often a result of still carrying things that you should have let go. It's easy to feel submerged with heaviness when the bulk of the burdens that you continue to uplift are the exact things that you need to lay aside.

In like manner, if the pain is old, let it go so that you can open up space for greater purpose and new opportunities. We have a hard time letting go because deep down inside, we fear that what we are losing is the best that we will ever have. This way of thinking is flawed. It is simply not true. I believe that what's ahead of you is bigger than you can even begin to imagine.

We must graduate from the grip of our history, so that we don't run the risk of aborting our destinies. We can no longer allow our family and friends to determine what's right for us. We can no longer depend on others for validation. I want you to know that you are enough. You have the emotional and mental strength to be self-sufficient and forward thinking.

We cannot use old solutions to solve new problems. Our grandmothers were strong women, but the truth is that they carried too much. There are so many emotional hang ups that they should've let go. Unfortunately, they didn't have the same resources that are afforded to us today. Their living conditions were rooted in a cultural crisis stemming from years of unhealed emotional injury. Generations of young girls are suffering the wounds of their grandmothers. When we choose to heal from hurt, we give future generations of women an example of what it is to be whole. Our children, and our children's children deserve to experience the world without the piercing fragments of broken hearts, tainted history and a limited vision on possibility.

 **STAR MOMENT**

Tasha Cobbs-Leonard

Grammy and Stellar Award winning artist, Tasha Cobbs-Leonard has been a pillar of strength, wisdom and courage in my life. I will never forget that week of bitter-sweet moments when this "Daddy's" girl lost her father suddenly. It was just a few days before winning her first Grammy. I marveled at her strength to accept what God allowed while delivering God's message of love. The way she was able to minister God's word right in the midst of her own grief was extremely admirable. Most people shut down, retreat, or avoid interaction which is completely understandable; but to see her minister so powerfully through song with a broken heart was a display of strength that only God could have given her. That level of resilience and perseverance is to be honored.

DEVOTIONAL PRAYER
FOR YOUR MAKEUP KIT

Prayer

Lord today I decree and declare That I will do the inner work required to Cleanse my soul of fear, un-forgiveness, regret, doubt and anxiety. Because None of these pollutants are healthy additives to my soul. Each of them tear me down "Peace by PEACE." And My inner PEACE matters! Lord help me to keep my mind on you because it Is in you where I find my Peace and the cleaner my thoughts are, the lighter I feel. And I will NOT allow my past to shatter my potential for total Beauty. I speak that today I am CLEANSED!

Notes and Reflections

_____

_____

_____

_____

_____

_____

_____

Soul Work

To Do List:

_____ ☐
_____ ☐
_____ ☐
_____ ☐
_____ ☐
_____ ☐
_____ ☐
_____ ☐
_____ ☐

Goals

_____

_____

_____

_____

_____

_____

_____

_____

_____

Today's Devotion

_____

_____

_____

_____

_____

_____

_____

_____

_____

_____

Personal Affirmations

_____

_____

_____

_____

_____

_____

_____

_____

_____

_____

Reflections

COMMANDMENT 3

Prep & Prime

"Thou shall prepare thyself daily with
worship, prayer while setting daily goals"

This chapter discusses Prepping of each day in order
to be mentally and spiritually successful!

In order to be prepped and primed for the day I must
incorporate these non-negotiable practices into my
routine.

Pro Tip

*The purpose of Priming products is to hold the foundation and other
colors in place. Otherwise when temperatures increase the products
may break down and separate.*

Prepping for my day means taking the time to read God's
word, mandating a moment to worship, and prioritizing
prayer and time to meditate. This 30 minute block begins
my day; my routine always takes place in the quiet of the

morning. If I know I have an early morning, I get up 30 minutes earlier. This 30 min block can never be compromised for me. You must remember how you start your day charts your day. Your prep and prime time holds the difficulties of the day together. No matter what heat I'm facing I'm more equipped to withstand the fire when I'm armed with worship, the word of God and meditation.

The purpose of priming products is to hold the foundation and other colors in place. Otherwise when temperatures increase, the products may break down and separate.

Allow great things to manifest by preparing your mind for all occurrences whether they are good or bad. Having a daily priming practice fills you with strength to deal with the battles of the day while giving you enough gratitude and grace to live through it, all while expecting the best possible outcome.

If we're not careful, we can allow bad occurrences to negatively influence us. It you don't properly regard your problems and imperfections, you will doubt who you are, and lose sight of what you've been called and created to do. The enemy throws things your way to make you feel less than. His job is to steal, kill and destroy your recollection of all of the good thoughts, good deeds and things that you've done right. By not spending the adequate time with God daily, I remember being low in spirit because I wasn't consistently doing the prep and prime work. So, when life seemed to fall apart, the enemy tormented me and I allowed it; because I wasn't praying, meditating or reading Gods promises. I had inadvertently given the enemy the power to enter with unauthorized access. I had surrendered my armor and become an easy target. My spirit wasn't fortified through prayer so the adversary had a gateway to get in. I started to doubt my talent and my services. One day in church, I activated my weapon of worship. What I know for sure, is that when we worship God, we evoke his presence. We summons Him to show up when we worship and call on His name. There were some achievements that God still had in store for me; and while I may have lost sight of His promises, He had not forgotten. I had lost my connection with him and as a result, I lost sight of the treasures He had for me. When you accept God's power, you uncover your true identity, but this process must be preceded with a sacred relationship.

Needless to say, I learned my lesson, and when I feel challenged in areas I increase my time with God in worship. Having an intimate relationship with God has been the formula for my success. Worship is different than just knowing scripture.

Just like having knowledge is one thing, while activating the power thereof is different. You can know how to fight, but lack the power to win the fight. Worship reactivates your power.

Hebrews 11:6 " But without faith it is impossible to please Him: for he that cometh to God must believe that He is, and that He is a rewarder of them that diligently seek Him."

⭐ STAR MOMENT ⭐

Erica Campbell

Early call times have been a part of my life for over 20 years. Who knew that in the Wee hours of the morning before the sun rises that so much work could be done while charting out the success of your day. If you think I'm talking about physical work you are sadly mistaken. I'm speaking specifically about SOUL work. Before there was "Get Up Mornings" with Erica Campbell which starts as early as 5am in some time zones, I witnessed this Grammy Award winning Artist begin her day with prayer, praise and devotions. It was such a joy traveling with Erica because I was able to witness the work she puts into her daily routine. And I truly believe this uncompromised regimen is the key to her success as an artist, wife, first lady and mother. As a pillar in the gospel community who ministers to thousands of souls daily, she truly understands the importance of spending quality time with GOD. Walking with and serving this angel has truly been one of my life's greatest joys.

DEVOTIONAL PRAYER
FOR YOUR MAKEUP KIT

"Lord As I prepare for today, I prime my thoughts with worship and quiet meditation. This time with you is valued and special to me. Your word declares that early in the morning should I seek thee. (Psalms 63). Lord, I don't know what today holds or what battles I may have to face but I trust in the Lord of my salvation to protect my heart and mind. And because I'm called to be a walking epistle of your word, I bring beauty and peace into all places of turmoil."

Notes and Reflections

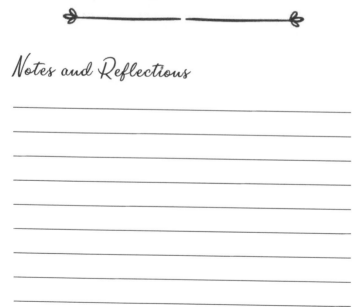

Soul Work

To Do List:

_____ ☐

_____ ☐

_____ ☐

_____ ☐

_____ ☐

_____ ☐

_____ ☐

_____ ☐

_____ ☐

Goals

_____

_____

_____

_____

_____

_____

_____

_____

_____

_____

Today's Devotion

_____
_____
_____
_____
_____
_____
_____
_____
_____
_____

Personal Affirmations

_____
_____
_____
_____
_____
_____
_____
_____
_____
_____
_____

Reflections

_____

_____

_____

_____

_____

_____

_____

_____

_____

_____

_____

_____

_____

_____

_____

_____

_____

_____

_____

_____

_____

_____

_____

COMMANDMENT 4

Foundation / Concealer

"Thou shall never forget that God's word
covers me in every situation."

My foundation is the word of God! It matches my
life perfectly. I never have to wonder how to apply
it. The word is accurate and it never lies.

My Foundation is solid and tailored specifically for me.

Whenever my feelings vary about myself, God's thoughts
of me never change. His word is definite and it is sure.

Because I am hand chosen by God, my thoughts and
feelings matter to Him.

Concealer is used to cover, and my spiritual concealer is
the Holy Spirit.

Pro Tip

*A foundation/ **concealer** or color corrector is a type of cosmetic that is used to mask dark circles, age spots, large pores, and other small blemishes visible on the skin. Both products hide different pigments by blending the imperfections into the surrounding skin tone causing the skin to appear even, smooth, and blemish free.*

"It is hard to add makeup to naked skin. foundation is similar to primer, it gives you something to build upon.

Priming gives you the ability to lay a foundation that allows you to conceal and cover your flaws. When you are applying primer, you are beginning with a clean slate; a bare face. During this stage of application you able to see the skin in its actual form. All flaws are apparent and you are aware of what needs to be concealed and accentuated. I've had people sit in my chair and assume that their skin needed more product than was actually necessary after watching a few youtube videos.

So often we amplify our flaws and apply more criticism than what is warranted based on unrealistic beauty standards upheld by popular culture and mainstream society.

Don't ever adopt a diminished sense of beauty based off of airbrushed and photoshopped propaganda. Learn who you and whose you are. God's word reminds us that we are fearfully and wonderfully made. We are perfectly imperfect and this is what makes us unique.

The priming stage of our journey entails battles with self-esteem and identity. During this time, we face the fear of standing out and not looking like everyone else.

When we coat ourselves with foundation, we internally lay down the blocks to build upon our personal power. The architectural framework of self-mastery gives us a solid stance to further develop as women, wives, mothers and daughters.

I can recall a time when I was working at BET. On this particular day, I made a request upon God. I did what His word instructed and I simply asked that He endowed me with the spirit of adequacy. I was stricken with fear that I was somehow inadequate and that my lack of experience would be exposed. I had to rely on the word of God in that moment to cover me. I had to remind myself that although I was entering rooms with great opportunities, it was God's favor and His hand on my life that had given me access in the first place. I became empowered when I realized that I didn't have to worry about if I had what it took to be successful in that instance because it is God who qualifies the called. The mere fact that I was working in such a prominent studio, was proof that God's grace was sufficient enough to allow me to prosper in the exact position that He had allowed me to be promoted to.

God can fill up any area where you lack. His essence is that of plenty and abundance.

Having a solid foundation births promise for your future. When your base is sturdy you can withstand the elements of life's changes. You are able to keep it together through transitional weather and seasonal shifts.

In order to win against the many worries of the world, you must be solid at your core. When you know that you are fearfully and wonderfully made, you don't crumble from the criticism of others. When you are secured in the sacredness of God's affection, you can stand tall even when the world around you feels like it's falling down. Your foundation is your strength. It is the presence of inner stamina that holds you up while you carry your dreams, your purpose and the many responsibilities in your life without faltering.

While foundation is our base, concealer is an additional solvent to veil problem areas.

Concealer is our unwavering reminder that God can take our ugly mess and still create a masterpiece. He can take our ugly past and give us a beautiful future.

Much like the story in Isaiah 61:3 where we learn the concept of beauty for ashes.

What we fail to realize is that in this story in the bible, there is an exchange taking place. You have to give God those burdens in exchange for His blessings.

There is a sense of healing that you will begin to experience when you give your problems, fears, doubts and concerns to God. When you give him your grief, He will give you beauty by way of peace and understanding.

You have to give something to get something. You have to give up your grief in order to obtain the glory and grace of God. He conceals our pain with the release of His Peace.

So, where should your mind be during grief? Pain? Hardship? While our default response is to focus on our pain, we must be intentional to keep our minds on God.

He will be the one to erase the scars that are etched in our souls.

This interaction is a valuable transaction. The trust factor is the formula for our salvation. No matter how dark or blemished our problem is, we must maintain and nurture the belief that God can and He will cover it. Stop punishing yourself for your ugly past, because God has covered it already.

We must be firm and understand that the world is ready for us but sometimes we're not ready for the world. We carry the fear that the world can still see our scars, even though God's word has assured us that He has blotted out our transgressions. So blot it out of your memory. Stop replaying failed scenarios in your head. Stop nursing it with fallible applications but work on yourself so that you can experience true healing. When you continue to focus on your failures, it prohibits you from moving forward. Know that God has already prepared you to do something great. He has already covered you and concealed your flaws. Now you must get out of your own way by forgiving yourself and moving forward.

We tend to harbor an attachment to broken things. We're holding on to old ideas of who we are, and working so hard to mask emotions that are no longer relevant in our lives. Much like when we apply concealer to areas that are no longer a problem only because we have become accustomed to our makeup routine. Chances are, you're covering things that people aren't even paying attention to. God has already covered you.

The world needs your gift not your attachment to your flaws. God can give you beauty but He may require that you give up the ashes.

Perhaps you are covering your insecurities around other powerful women with the excuse that you don't get along with women. Perhaps you are concealing your inability to confront conflict with your nature to avoid them all together. You will never be able to conquer what you're unwilling to confront. Challenge yourself to see the truth in your ways, even if it means having enough courage to recognize where you went wrong so that you can be better in that area.

 **STAR MOMENT**

Serita Jakes

Serita Jakes was my first "celebrity" client over 25 years ago. We were introduced by my former pastors at an annual New Year's revival service in Washington D.C where her husband, Bishop T.D Jakes was the guest speaker. I was a law student at the time but had a vested interest in beauty because my family owned a popular full service salon. I remember the day Lady Jakes walked into the salon how excited we all were to service Bishop's gorgeous wife. After her coif was complete I offered to add a little makeup as a finishing touch. If I recall, it was only a little powder and lipstick, but boy was she happy with the end result! I remember her face like it was yesterday but more importantly I remember her words of encouragement. She told me that my hands were anointed while speaking GOD's words of favor over my life. She said I would go to the nations and share my gift with the world, and that moment changed my life forever. I will never forget that moment because every word she spoke has come to pass. God's word is so inspiring and those that carry His word in their hearts are a treasure.

DEVOTIONAL PRAYER
FOR YOUR MAKEUP KIT

"Lord I thank you for covering me with your promises.
Your word is a blueprint to the success of my salvation.
My hope is built on your word; because your word never
lies and it never fails." (Joshua 21:45)

Notes and Reflections

Soul Work

To Do List:

_____ ☐

_____ ☐

_____ ☐

_____ ☐

_____ ☐

_____ ☐

_____ ☐

_____ ☐

_____ ☐

Goals

_____

_____

_____

_____

_____

_____

_____

_____

_____

_____

Today's Devotion

_____

_____

_____

_____

_____

_____

_____

_____

_____

Personal Affirmations

_____

_____

_____

_____

_____

_____

_____

_____

_____

_____

Reflections

_____

_____

_____

_____

_____

_____

_____

_____

_____

_____

_____

_____

_____

_____

_____

_____

_____

_____

_____

_____

_____

_____

_____

_____

_____

_____

COMMANDMENT 5

Contour / Highlight

"Thou shall learn to cut away things that are not needed while accentuating the needed things in my life."

Pro Tip

Highlighting is blending a lighter shade of makeup on certain parts of your face in order to bring attention to them. i.e, the upper part of your cheekbones, bridge if your nose, chin, cupid's bow, center of your forehead and other areas that you would want to stand out more than usual.

Unlike the parts of us that we want to conceal, cover and even cut away; there is a part of us that glows and produces an inner shimmer. These are the pieces of who we are that we are more comfortable with showing off. It represents our strong suit, our good attributes, our strengths, our innate gifts, and our talents.

Each of us possess something on the inside of us that is just waiting for the opportunity to shine outwardly. The things we are passionate about and the things that bring us the most fulfillment are the exact things that illuminate from within. It's what makes our souls attractive. It's what others feel when they interact with or experience as we operate in our gifts.

While we are all a work in progress, it's so important that as we work on ourselves, we are mindful to celebrate and highlight the parts of ourselves and the part of our lives that represent our strengths as we do the work to become better in the areas where we may fall short.

The world responds with enthusiasm to things that glow. So, shine bright. When I consider my career in the beauty industry and even my insight on product inventory, what I know is that highlighter products amongst various makeup brands, tend to be the highest selling product. This is an indicator that people are naturally attracted to light.

So, be the light! Accentuate the light that you possess. Take time to consider what is it that you do well. When are you at your happiest? When do you feel most fulfilled?

Look over your life, maybe even scroll through a photo album, your Facebook photos or Instagram timeline, As you review the photos at different stages of your life, what images stand out to you? Which moments would you revisit if you were able to? When were you at your best? What was going on in your life when you were at your happiest? What were the moments in your life that you are most proud of? What have you accomplished over your life? What moments brought you the most joy? Was it a beautiful wedding? The birth of a child? Graduating from college? Maybe witnessing your child or grandchild graduate, Did you buy a home? Did you reach your weight loss goal? Did you start a business? Write a book?

We tend to focus too much on the negative things in our lives, so much so that we lose sight of all of the many blessings and joyous moments that have shaped our memories.

If you're anything like most people on the planet, you have things that you want to work on and even things that you are downright unhappy with in your life. As you develop the tools to become better, heal from brokenness and gain power over your past; I want you to become empowered by developing your highlight reel. This simple activity is a highly impactful exercise in gratitude. It creates a shift in your spirit and your focus. It allows you to see yourself, your life and even the situation you're working and growing through in a whole new light. When you shift your perspective you in turn change your whole world.

I want you to make a collage of photos that show you in your highest essence. Choose the photos, videos or other insignia that truly represent your best life. It can be a digital collage for those who are tech savvy, or an old school cut out and paste on a whiteboard for those who prefer a more hands on experience.

Whatever your preference, I want you to have some fun with this. Maybe even invite some friends over to join in on the fun. You can even write honest reviews on one another's strengths and gifts. Sometimes it's healthy to know how others perceive you. We can be our own worst critic. Life beats us up enough, we have to be intentional about uplifting ourselves and others.

 **STAR MOMENT**

Cecily Tyson

I was reminded of the importance of highlighting and capturing great moments after a full day of festivities during the world-renowned Essence festival in New

Orleans. I was working with the legendary Cecily Tyson. She is most known for her epic portrayal of strong black women in movies such as The Help and The Autobiography of Miss Jane Pittman. Cecily has a presence that is so strong, yet still so meek. The aura that she carries is both powerful and filled with wisdom that you can only acquire from living life in its full quintessence.

Cecily is the type of woman who has a quietness about her, yet when she opens her mouth, everything around her settles in order to take in what she has to say. When she speaks, it's an impartation of wisdom and grace.

After a long day of interviews, meet and greets, photo ops, and interaction with fans, peers and colleagues, I knew that the 94-year-old icon was a bit exhausted. If I'm speaking honestly, I was tired too. As we were driving in the car, Cicely broke the silence with a question. She said, in her sultry voice, "Kym, do you have a diary?"

"No" I replied softly.

She said, "Kym, you are traveling with a legend. These are the type of memories that you should never forget"

Then it hit me, how often do we take moments for granted? I mean, here I am riding in a luxury SUV with Cicely Tyson, for me I had become accustomed to high profile clients, but I had lost sight of just how special and how significant the opportunities I was blessed with were. It's not every day that people get to work with clients who they love, admire, look up to and can learn from. I mean, how many other people could say, "I'm riding in a car alongside Cicely Tyson"

You see, I had set my focus so much on where I was going in the future, the goals I was working to achieve and the next thing that I wanted to accomplish, and as a result I was missing out on the magic that was happening in my life in the present moment.

After that conversation, I started to think, what are the moments in my life that I never want to forget? So I started scrolling through old pictures in my phone, and each picture tells a different story about the woman I was at that time. I immediately started to feel a strong sense of gratitude. I looked back and realized that I had a bright highlight reel.

I stopped and thanked God for the collective moments of greatness throughout the years. It eased my anxiety for the future because I realized that God had been with me along the way. During my ups and my downs, my behind the scenes pain and even my life highlights. God was right there in the midst of it all. He had never left me and I know that He is with you too. When you look back, you will see how He has kept you. Perhaps you may be anxious to relocate from the home you're living in, but when you look back, you may remember that the same home you've grown tired of, is the same home you prayed for and received. Life is all about perspective. How will you choose to view your life and your current situation? Will you focus on the pain and the things that you cannot change? Or will you take a moment to express gratitude for all the goodness God has shown you throughout the course of your life.

It's not your situation that will keep you stuck, it's how you see your situation that will liberate you or keep you in bondage. For instance, you may not hit your revenue goals every day; but while it may not be your best day financially, it may still be a day that you are in great health.

As we move on to contouring, I want you to consider what needs to be cut away in your life?

Contouring is temporary, it's not permanent. You have to know when it's time to cut things out of your life.

When to say no to certain opportunities and certain activities. It's so critical to know when to walk away, when to release and when to let go.

Highlighting focuses on the things that you we can illuminate for maximum allure, while contouring speaks to what we may need to cut out in order to shine brighter.

When we focus too much on our problems, we tend to notice more of them, but when we celebrate and express gratitude for the things that are going well in our lives we then expand our perspective for possibilities.

DEVOTIONAL PRAYER
FOR YOUR MAKEUP KIT

Lord your word teaches us that in EVERYTHING we are to give thanks. (1 Thessalonians 5:18)   So help me to appreciate and cherish all the highlights in my life. Even when the dark moments seem to hover over my head, allow my focus to be on what you've done for me, and all the blessings you have given me. Release me from my need to worry about the things I'm waiting on from you.

Help me to realize that you are developing me and shaping me and that you are never destroying me. Your name is Emmanuel and you never leave me nor forsake me. So I know that if you're with me I will have peace, love and comfort. I will stand on your word that says, "All things are working together for my good, because I am called according to your purpose. (Romans 8:28)

Notes and Reflections

Soul Work

To Do List:

_____ ☐
_____ ☐
_____ ☐
_____ ☐
_____ ☐
_____ ☐
_____ ☐
_____ ☐
_____ ☐

Goals

_____
_____
_____
_____
_____
_____
_____
_____
_____

Today's Devotion

_____

_____

_____

_____

_____

_____

_____

_____

_____

Personal Affirmations

_____

_____

_____

_____

_____

_____

_____

_____

_____

_____

Reflections

_____

_____

_____

_____

_____

_____

_____

_____

_____

_____

_____

_____

_____

_____

_____

_____

_____

_____

_____

_____

_____

_____

_____

COMMANDMENT 6

Brows

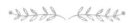

"Thou shall always remember that my frame
is important and serves a purpose"

This chapter explains the importance of recognizing your framing. The core of who you are and how you are made. It teaches you how to celebrate your unique personality and to never compromise your hearts desires to fit someone else's mold.

Eyebrows have a similar purpose as it relates to the construction of the face. I affectionately call eyebrows the "Swiss Army Knife" of the human body—they do everything! First and foremost, they protect your eyes. The shape of the brow ridge and the brows themselves channel sweat, rain, and moisture away from the eyeballs so that your vision stays clear.

Secondly, our eyebrows are essential for nonverbal **communication**; and finally, they are a **frame** to your face. Their unique shape is the personality of your facial features.

Pro Tip

By learning the correct methods and techniques for shaping your eyebrows, you'll be able to create the most flattering appearance for your face.

Eyebrows frame the face, when it's off, it changes the composition of the face.

The trend of eyebrows has changed drastically through the years. Current eyebrow trends may have been frowned upon in previous years as you may well have noticed with each decade the size and shape of your brows may have changed. If you don't believe me, pull out a few old photos of yourself. While observing these photos notice the change in your physical appearance and even your countenance. Many of our old photos tell the story of our framing and where we were in life. Whether we were in our happiest moments or experiencing times of sorrow or regret.

We must remember that when the framing is off, people will misjudge you based on how you appear. So, what does your framing say? Are you stand-off-ish, arrogant, unapproachable, or simply a mean girl? These personality flaws can be the cause of some of your rejection ; but like the eye brows this can easily be changed with a little adjustment. Then there are other times when our placement is off. We are out of line with Gods plan for our lives. When you're in the right place at the wrong time, or the right time, and the wrong place,

There's a sense of timing and framing that God orders and it's His divine order. When you're out of frame, you are out of the umbrella of where He wants you to be. If you're careful and using discernment, you'll get wet in a season where God's plan was for you to be covered.

I've had moments when customers/ clients don't respond to your offer, it could be that what you're offering may not fit their current needs, you could be out of season. It's possible to have the right product with the wrong audience, or even the right product, with the right audience but at the wrong time.

Eyebrows are to enhance while eyelashes are designed to be a protectant. It's a forecast of your eyes; they naturally protect your eyes.

When the Holy Spirit gives you a warning, it acts as a protectant to keep danger out. This is why discernment is so critical.

As you continue to show up in life as the highest version of who you are, the way in which you are internally shaped will be revealed in your ability to own your uniqueness. This represents the distinctive way in which you operate from your core belief system along with the understanding of your individual purpose. It is the outline for how every other component in your life should be designed. This sets the standard and the style from which all other adornments should align. When a makeup artist designs someone's eyebrows, they are sure to consider how every other additive must fit within the supporting structure of our facial frame. You usually don't ever see the evidence of eyeshadow extend beyond the eyebrow profile.

When I consider facial framing through eyebrow production, I think of the boundaries that we must have in place to ensure that we show up as our best selves. When your eyebrows are off, it can throw off your entire look, just like when your barriers are not established, you find yourself frazzled, stressed and stretched thin from an overload of obligations pulling you in too many directions at once.

We don't realize the significance of implementing barriers to limit access until we are overwhelmed with the consequences of failing to do so. You have the power to determine what serves you and what is not a good fit. There will be things in your life that may have once served a purpose but they have reached the end of their shelf line, and just like the expired parts of your life that you must be courageous enough to dump, you must also employ wisdom to know what needs to be added. The cool thing about boundaries, is that while it allows us to protect ourselves from the things we do not want in our lives, it empowers us to pick and choose what we can implement to make our lives better. This could be hiring an assistant to delegate responsibilities to so that our business and home affairs operate more smoothly. Or even hiring a personal trainer to lead and guide your physical fitness, or even a chef who is better able to prepare healthy meals. Setting the framework for your life details the construct from which you are internally governed.

 **STAR MOMENT**

Ledisi

One of the most admired qualities a celebrity can possess is the ability to create boundaries while maintaining a life of structure. I was blessed to travel around the world with Grammy nominated artist Ledisi and she has mastered this trait. While pouring out her heart and soul each night during her tour, I grew to appreciate her tenacious ability to maintain a level of consistent self-renewal. Adequate rest proved to be her secret weapon while studying her craft tenaciously. No tempting activities ever caused her to compromise her coveted voice or performances. Each nights standing ovations proved that her methods truly worked.

DEVOTIONAL PRAYER
FOR YOUR MAKEUP KIT

"Lord help me to be steadfast, immovable and always abounding in your work. Lead and guide me when I am tempted to fail or fall. I know that there is nothing too hard for you. Help me to be solid like a rock while standing firmly on your word."

Notes and Reflections

_____

_____

_____

_____

_____

_____

_____

_____

_____

_____

_____

_____

Soul Work

To Do List:

_____ ☐
_____ ☐
_____ ☐
_____ ☐
_____ ☐
_____ ☐
_____ ☐
_____ ☐
_____ ☐

Goals

_____
_____
_____
_____
_____
_____
_____
_____
_____
_____

Today's Devotion

_____

_____

_____

_____

_____

_____

_____

_____

_____

_____

Personal Affirmations

_____

_____

_____

_____

_____

_____

_____

_____

_____

_____

_____

Reflections

_____

_____

_____

_____

_____

_____

_____

_____

_____

_____

_____

_____

_____

_____

_____

_____

_____

_____

_____

_____

_____

_____

_____

COMMANDMENT 7

Eye makeup

"Thou shall see NEXT with NOW eyes"

This chapter discusses our present state. Often times we can become discouraged because of what we see now! From our weight, to our finances, our hair and even our love life. Every day presents a different challenge. Some days we can be drowned with all of these occurrences at the same time

I am encouraging you to see yourself from a different vantage point. I emphasize that we are all a work in progress.

In the physical sense, there are so many eye-shapes and shades to adorn our eyes for every occasion. The Makeup selections and applications are endless and because of limitless options the consumer can become overwhelmed.

Take the time to learn your eye-shape and what colors best compliment you.

Pro Tip

Eye shadow is a cosmetic that is applied on the eyelids and under the eyes. It is commonly used to make the wearer's eyes stand out or look more attractive. Eye shadow can add depth and dimension to one's eyes, compliment one's eye color, make one's eyes appear larger, or simply draw attention to the eyes.

Eyeshadow

Depending on the eye size, you can create custom looks to obtain a desired outcome by adding color usually in a powder form for the purpose of accentuating the eyes and face. It is commonly used to make the wearers eyes stand out or look more attractive.

The parallel is that these are the extra things that we should be adding to our lives in order to experience increased joy. And I call these "Extra" practices Self-care! Self-care means you're finally giving yourself the attention that YOU NEED. Some of the self-care practices that we implement as well as the wellness techniques that we invest in enable us to mandate time to be at our best. We know that self-care is a priority, but eyeshadow represents when we go the extra mile to adorn our look and be at our best. This is about going deeper and gaining a better understanding of your unique qualities. Discovering what sets you apart, what makes you stand out, what looks good on you and what is it that you really like. I've had clients request a smokey eye or a cat eye because it was the trend at the time, but after having that particular technique applied, they found that they didn't like the way it looked on them. Sure it looked great on the model in the ad, but often times, clients don't fully consider if a trend truly suits their features and personal style. How often do we find ourselves caught up doing things that we really don't enjoy, simply because, dare I say it? "Everyone else is doing it."

Imagine just how much power you harness when you resist the urge to go with the flow, and you take a stand for your own desires. Imagine leaving your job prematurely because of the influx and glamorization of entrepreneurship, only to discover that you aren't mentally and emotionally suited to be in business for yourself. Imagine being stressed out at the beginning and end of every month when you don't have the funds to cover your expenses, only to discover that your work ethic and your crave for stability was better suited for a job. I see this happen so often. We get caught up in the hype and we fail to consider what God had in mind when he created us. What was His vision for your life when He breathed air into your lungs? God's will is overshadowed by the demands and ever changing trends in society. We are all trying to keep up, when in actuality, we should be focusing on discovering our divine pace and celebrating our personal space to develop.

Your eyes are symbolic of your perspective. It is significant to have clarity regarding how you see yourself and how you view your situation. Is what you're seeing and what you're living lining up? What are the things that are influencing your vision? Is your vision being hindered due to you viewing your life through someone else's lens? Do you have a clear eye view? These are the questions that you must ask yourself often in order to recalibrate and stay connected to God's vision for your life.

⭐ STAR MOMENT ⭐

Whitney Houston

I remember working on set with singer and actress Whitney Houston, this was after she had faced public scrutiny, criticism and a slew of widespread harsh opinion from the media. Although she was getting back to work, her personal sense of esteem had been affected by the negative media attention. This was evident when a group of fans approached her on set. They were elated to see her and they approached her with enthusiasm, praise and celebration. I was shocked when I realized how she was a bit taken aback by their response. Once the fans went on their way, I asked her why she had responded to their praise with such surprise. In my mind, I couldn't understand why she would not expect such enthusiasm from fans, after all, she was "Whitney Houston". She expressed to me that after experiencing a great deal of bad press, she didn't think that the general public still loved and accepted her despite her public trials and struggles. At that moment, I had a profound epiphany. I realized then that the way we see ourselves is often heavily influenced by how we think others perceive us. Whitney Houston was an icon but her sense of self had become a bit tainted by public opinion. This reminded me of God's love, His grace and His mercy. What if we gave ourselves the same grace that God gives us? No matter how many times we fall short, He still sees the best of us. His grace is sufficient enough to cover all of our transgressions so that we may continue to grow and heal without guilt or shame. Whitney has gone down in history as one of the best to ever do it. She is literally a legend. Her struggle does not eliminate the power of her gift or the reach of her talent, and neither does yours.

DEVOTIONAL PRAYER
FOR YOUR MAKEUP KIT

"Lord My eyes are the mirrors to my soul. Today I'm trusting you to help me to see My NEXT with NOW Eye's. With your help, EYE won't allow what I see to hinder me from my next. My weight, my hair, my skin, my facial features. Everyday EYE will work on being and SEEING myself HAPPY and WHOLE."

Notes and Reflections

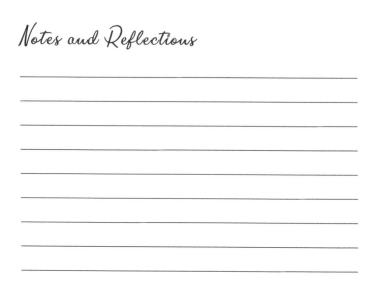

Soul Work

To Do List:

_____ ☐
_____ ☐
_____ ☐
_____ ☐
_____ ☐
_____ ☐
_____ ☐
_____ ☐
_____ ☐

Goals

_____
_____
_____
_____
_____
_____
_____
_____
_____

Today's Devotion

_____

_____

_____

_____

_____

_____

_____

_____

_____

Personal Affirmations

_____

_____

_____

_____

_____

_____

_____

_____

_____

_____

Reflections

_____

_____

_____

_____

_____

_____

_____

_____

_____

_____

_____

_____

_____

_____

_____

_____

_____

_____

_____

_____

_____

_____

_____

_____

_____

COMMANDMENT 8

Lips

"Thou shall only speak positivity
from my lips."

During this chapter I emphasize the importance of watching our language! We must remember that our current declarations determine our Future manifestations!

Pro Tip

Lipstick is a cosmetic product containing pigments, oils, waxes, and emollients that apply color, texture and protection to the lips.

"Death and Life are in the power of our tongues"

The same way that we take the time adorn our lips with beautiful colors and textures we must take the same efforts to tailor our words.

Whether it's birthing a new business or the funeral of a bad habit. Our words have power! Can you imagine the powerful things that we could do if we simply learned how to discipline our tongues. I once heard someone reference our tongues as "Pink Tornados' because of the treacherous words swirling from it. Our self-destructing words can potentially ruin relationships with others and sabotage opportunities. We must always consider that the words we choose can spark up ambition and confidence or they can cause us to feel anxious and inadequate. "The words you speak become the house you live in." Your language also impacts how others see you and relate to you. When you feel undervalued or overlooked I challenge you to do a 24-hour tongue fast! No ungodly conversations and NO negative words shall be tolerated.

Like the scripture states, "And you will eat the fruit of what you say". (Proverbs 18:21)

We either render ourselves as powerful or powerless!

We are change agents assigned to shift the spiritual atmosphere anywhere we set our feet. We are marketplace agents and through us God is going to manifest miracles! God requires us to use our words wisely as we progress in life. Never forget the power of your words. If you're wondering WHY certain things haven't manifested, take an inventory of your words. Create a conversation with yourself and speak well of your current state. Proactively recite GOD's word over every negative situation. Remember God has an expected end for you. Jeremiah 29:11 is one of my favorite scriptures and I reference it often when the odds seem to stack up against me. For every "Goliath" moment in my life I recite this scripture.

"For I know the plans I have for you, DECLARES the Lord… Plans to prosper you and not to harm you, plans to give you hope and a future."

Just knowing that GOD has a PLAN for us gives me so much hope even when I don't have a "plan of my own." When life throws us a curveball and our plans seem to shatter, always remember that GOD has the ultimate plan. Don't forfeit your future by speaking negatively about certain phases in life. "Self-Talk" is a huge part of what makes us who we are. Our words can impact how we feel, the things we can achieve in life, how we interact with others and how we're viewed by the world. When we implement healthier word choice, we also reduce stress. We have all heard the metaphor that references how we view a glass; is it half full or half empty? Our words have the propensity to impact our self-image, self-esteem, and our confidence.

⭐ STAR MOMENT ⭐

Bozoma St. John

Have you ever met a person who always knows exactly what to say? No matter the circumstances or the problems, they seem to have a comforting solution. They tend to always know exactly what to say and when to say it. If there was a badge of honor given to anyone for possessing this gift it would go to Bozoma St. John. This 6-foot tall power house, and style maven is so much more than beauty and fashion. She is one of the smartest women I know in the PR and marketing space. As a trail blazing, brand marketing executive, she has represented companies like Beats by Dre, Uber and William Morris. I met Boz 6 years ago after the passing of her husband and her words to me are still ringing in my ears. She told me without hesitation that she was determined to live her life fearlessly and boldly. At the time, She was transitioning to the west coast with a small child. She was taking on a new career as a widow; and without any apprehension, she spoke her future into existence. She said, "Kym I will make it to the top because cream always rises. As long as I have God on my side, I can do anything but fail!" Just recently I was able to visit with her while in Los Angeles and she is still rising. She continues to speak abundance over her life and to all whom she encounters. Surround yourselves with people who speak with life enhancing verbiage so that you can soak up each word during moments when you need to be resuscitated.

DEVOTIONAL PRAYER
FOR YOUR MAKEUP KIT

"Lord your word declares that death and life are in the power of my tongue and that I will EAT the fruit of what I say (Proverbs 18:21). Help me to speak sweetly and Peaceably over myself, my flaws, my family, my mate, my children, and anyone assigned to my life. My words are a weapon, and with your help I will use them to protect and not to destroy. My assignment matters and I will NOT abort your promises using sabotaging words." In Jesus name… amen!

Notes and Reflections

_____

_____

_____

_____

_____

_____

_____

_____

_____

Soul Work

To Do List:

	☐
	☐
	☐
	☐
	☐
	☐
	☐
	☐
	☐

Goals

Today's Devotion

_____

_____

_____

_____

_____

_____

_____

_____

_____

Personal Affirmations

_____

_____

_____

_____

_____

_____

_____

_____

_____

Reflections

_____

_____

_____

_____

_____

_____

_____

_____

_____

_____

_____

_____

_____

_____

_____

_____

_____

_____

_____

_____

_____

_____

COMMANDMENT 9

Blush

"Thou shall adorn thyself with beautiful
things, and we must do it often"

After painting thousands of faces, the one product many women could take or leave is blush.

In a nutshell, **blush** is used to add a flush of color to the cheeks, while bronzer is intended to make the skin look sun-kissed or tan. I'm always eager to encourage this step because a touch of color enhances the sentiment of the face. Blush can literally make you look innocent, or diva-esque. I always ask my clients which look they want to achieve.

Pro Tip

Blush, also referred to as Rouge, is a cosmetic for coloring the cheeks in varying shades, or the lips red. It is often applied as a powder or cream.

This chapter is one of my favorites! This is about the extra self-care moments we often neglect ourselves of. They are not necessarily needed for immediate survival but they are certainly an additive to complete our happiness and wholeness. Taking the time to examine your mind, body, and spirit to see what would make each entity flourish is an act of self-love and will expand your brain to its total beauty. Remember self-care is not selfish.

Adding Some of these things to your normal routine include:

1. Taking a hot bubble bath with candles.

2. Getting a Spa Pedicure.

3. Honoring your body with a massage.

4. Reading a blog for pleasure.

5. Journaling your dreams.

6. Going on a retreat alone.

7. Taking on a new hobby.

8. Doing something that scares you (skydiving, swimming in the ocean, roller skating)

9. Watching a funny movie and laughing.

10. Making your favorite dessert from scratch.

⭐ STAR MOMENT ⭐

Angela Bassett

Angela Bassett is celebrated as one of the most influential women in Hollywood, both mainstream and among her African American counterparts. She is best known for the roles that she has played depicting strong black women, and the timeless beauty she possesses in each role. Her physical physique is admired and sought after by many. Angela, not only looks good in film and print, but her beauty radiates in person as well. She is a master of prioritizing her needs while honoring her preservation. During the interim of serving as her makeup artist on the set of various movies and other productions that she's been employed for, I've been able to witness first-hand the personal power that she maintains to put herself first unapologetically. She has expanded my vernacular for true self-care. I have witnessed how she places her needs before all other obligations. She knows that when she is at her best, the world can receive the best version of her gifts and contributions. I can remember being impressed by her personal fortitude when turning down what I thought was a great opportunity. As she respectfully declined the offer, I wondered to myself why she had not accepted it.

Curious, I inquired and her answer floored me. She stated that the opportunity would conflict with the time she had already arranged for her self-care regimen. She made herself a priority, scheduled in time to give herself what she needed and placed a mandate on it. I was inspired to take the same non-negotiable approach with my own needs, values and desires.

DEVOTIONAL PRAYER FOR YOUR MAKEUP KIT

"Lord, help me to appreciate myself and the space you have me in. Help me to remember that my mind, body and spirit must be fortified DAILY. Help me to remember that I am responsible for the maintenance of my Mind and Soul. My life is a gift from you Lord and I will cherish every moment of it by handling it with SELF-Care!! Amen"

Notes and Reflections

_____

_____

_____

_____

_____

_____

_____

_____

_____

_____

_____

Soul Work

To Do List:

_____ ☐

_____ ☐

_____ ☐

_____ ☐

_____ ☐

_____ ☐

_____ ☐

_____ ☐

_____ ☐

Goals

Today's Devotion

_____

_____

_____

_____

_____

_____

_____

_____

_____

Personal Affirmations

_____

_____

_____

_____

_____

_____

_____

_____

_____

_____

Reflections

_____

_____

_____

_____

_____

_____

_____

_____

_____

_____

_____

_____

_____

_____

_____

_____

_____

_____

_____

_____

_____

_____

_____

_____

COMMANDMENT 10

Setting Spray

"Thou shall remember that there is power in being covered by the Blood of Jesus it is my protection"

This chapter ensures us of God's protection over our lives.

There was a study conducted by the University of Texas that indicates that 76% of women feel better about themselves when they feel protected by a spouse, father, or friend.

Pro Tip

Setting spray is also known as finishing spray. It is a cosmetic product designed to preserve applied make up for prolonged periods of time.

As Christian leaders we teach our congregations to rest in knowing that Jesus' blood was shed to remove the sins of the world for all who put their faith in Him.

Our faith to believe that everything we do in His name is covered by His power.

I believe that there is no entity of persecution, no self-destruction, or any caliber of negative self-talk that shall separate me from my purpose in life with the grace of God rebounding every oppressive trait.

Words will come, thoughts will come, things will happen, and we must know that we are protected by the blood of Jesus and that his protection for us can sometimes lead to rejection from others.

Metaphorically, I view setting spray as a protector of our face as it shields our makeup from the elements (heat and moisture) and it also helps to prevent smudging, and smearing after you apply a beautiful face. Keeping in mind that this product and process is much different from the primer; which holds it all together —the setting spray protects you from the after effects of the day.

In like manner, the blood of Jesus is used to protect us from words and actions that come in to destroy every prayer. The powerful blood of Jesus covers all the work you're doing daily to maintain your BRAIN BEAUTY! It's sealing everything we have taken the time to build.

Having a strong foundation will ensure that what you're building, creating and growing in, is being established on solid ground. Much like the makeup application process, what you start with is critical but how you finish is just as profound. The prime and foundation process is the preparation phase; it's what you do before you start to build while the setting spray phase is the final step that seals and protects what you've created. The setting spray phase speaks to the importance of having a covering.

I've been a makeup maven for many years, my experience and longevity in the beauty industry has allowed me to witness various trends in the market. The quality of products has evolved, marketing strategy fads have come, gone and resurfaced, and even the culture of the industry has experienced a great deal of transition.

In recent years, makeup manufacturers have changed the ingredients and the components of various products. In an attempt to build business through various product creation, companies started to break down the ingredients in the makeup formula in order to sell them separately.

There was a time when you could apply your makeup and it would stay in place all day without any additional products needing to be applied; but because elements have been removed, you now have to be intentional about utilizing a separate product to achieve long wear.

In an age where our society has become consumed with beauty standards, makeup company sales continue to thrive which is a great indicator of just how much value we place on how we look on the outside. We go through great lengths to "look the part" and it's almost second nature to purchase and consume the products that aid us in establishing our looks. Our makeup regimens and morning routines consist of many steps including applying a sealant such as a setting or finishing spray. Whether you are a fellow makeup artist, or just someone who enjoys the artistic transformation that makeup application provides, you understand the value and need to seal and set your makeup in order to experience lasting results. This concept is true in our personal lives as well.

Challenges, distractions, hardships, fears, doubt and self-imposed limited thinking are the things we face daily that attempt to break us down as we are building our lives, building our careers and growing in our spiritual maturity. Just like using a setting spray to seal all of the layers of a professional makeup application, it's important to have a covering over your life to shield and set in place the many things that God is using in your life to build you.

You too need a covering. Some added protective barrier to keep things in place and hold them all together. Having a covering protects you when you experience moments in life when you are vulnerable and your guard is down. Your mind and your spirit must be covered in prayer.

People who experience a breakdown have usually experienced some level of infiltration. Something has seeped in, or has been removed and now things are out of place. Much like when you're applying your makeup and you decide to skip the setting spray, so by midday your makeup is oily and smeared; when you skip a critical part of the process and you fail to cover, your makeup is not protected against the elements of your environment. So the conditions around you can penetrate with ease when there is no barrier of protection and the ingredient that keeps things together has been removed.

We must maintain an active relationship with God. We must be sure that while there are so many things fighting for our attention, that we don't allow God's influence in our lives to be removed. When we lack connection with God our lives suffer, much like when the sealing spray is removed from our makeup routine and the durability of our look is compromised. The setting spray saturates and seals everything that it touches and it creates a barrier between the elements. When we stay at God's feet in prayer, and we make meditation a practice, we are better able to hear and recognize God's voice. He gives us instruction and He covers us in His mercy, His protection and His grace.

You need a covering to protect what you're building. Since we don't have control over some of the elements that are present in our world that can infiltrate, damage and even destroy our dreams, our goals, our visions and even our families; we must be diligent in making sure we have protection in place to help sustain us during trying times that serve to protect our spirit and our minds.

In life, we sometimes experience loss, even when we are faithful in our prayers and active in our relationship building with Christ. The key is remembering that we are protected even during loss.

If you fail to cover your finances and you fail to bring order to your spending, when you don't have protection over your wealth in terms of financial literacy, you run the risk of losing your home, going broke or experiencing bankruptcy. Having financial advisors and mentors who have obtained financial success, or education on wealth acquisition is a covering that works to prevent financial brokenness. While these things may prevent most conflicts in this regard, there are certain challenges that are inevitable. In the event that you do lose, just remember that you can always get it back. God is a restorer. Just like a makeup wipe removes makeup from our faces and allows us to start all over again, God can give us a clean slate. You can always start fresh and build again.

We cannot allow the enemy to trick us into believing that material things are not replaceable. We have to stop measuring beauty through the lens of bundles and Bugatti's. Don't ever think that you need material things, unnecessary fluff, or a man to feel adequate. When we are not covered in self-esteem, we lack self-worth. When we fail to recognize our worth, we fall prey to accepting any old thing masquerading as love, attention or affection.

You must guard your heart, mind and your spirit by treating it as the valuable commodity that it is. Have a stable mind. In over 50 scriptures in the bible, it talks about the mind. This is how we know that mental wellness is so important. We must work to protect, fortify and enhance our minds. This means filtering what we allow in. We allow the opinions of others, social media, and other outside factors to distract and influence us too easily. In this day and age, we allow people into the sacred space of our minds with less resistance than we do allowing them into our homes. We have to stop allowing opinions and posts to govern our emotions. If we consume too much outside noise, it begins to influence how we see ourselves as well as how we see the world. It becomes a threat to our vision.

 STAR MOMENT

Omarosa Manigault-Newman

I remember reading the comments under a social media post that one of my clients had shared. I saw all of the negative, mean and nasty comments from internet trolls who did not even know her. I immediately began to pray for her. I prayed for a covering over her mind that she would not allow the unsolicited negative comments to take root in her mind, alter her mood or ruin her day.

This particular client (Omarosa Manigault-Newman) dealt with a lot of tough life occurrences and backlash because of her political alliance with President Trump. Her affiliation and support of the Republican party specifically President Trump, caused the black community to ostracize and cancel her. While I have not always agreed with her actions, what I admired about her was that despite how anyone felt about her, she was able to masterfully navigate through negativity, attack, backlash and even drama. She was heavily guarded and covered by her husband, loved ones and other trusted individuals who had been vetted. They covered her in prayer and in council.

She kept her circle tight with people who she knew meant her well, even those of us who didn't agree with her but still rallied in prayer to protect and cover her.

What I learned from watching Omarosa survive attacks and maintain her mental and emotional strength through opposition, was how the qualifier for massive success is in large part how well we can withstand trouble.

Omarosa survived that stage in her career because she knew who she could depend on and who she could call. She limited access to those wanting to connect with her and she got very clear about who was really for her. She was always so intentional about assessing the character and the level of integrity of those she allowed around her. This is the type of covering we need in our spiritual lives as well.

DEVOTIONAL PRAYER
FOR YOUR MAKEUP KIT

"God I thank you for the BLOOD! I thank you for covering me when I cannot cover myself. You are all knowing and ALL powerful. I am convinced that nothing can ever separate me from your love. Neither death nor life, neither angels nor demons, neither our fears for today nor our worries about tomorrow—not even the powers of hell can separate me from your love and your purpose for my life"

Notes and Reflections

Soul Work

To Do List:

_____ ☐
_____ ☐
_____ ☐
_____ ☐
_____ ☐
_____ ☐
_____ ☐
_____ ☐
_____ ☐

Goals

_____
_____
_____
_____
_____
_____
_____
_____
_____
_____

Today's Devotion

_____

_____

_____

_____

_____

_____

_____

_____

_____

_____

Personal Affirmations

_____

_____

_____

_____

_____

_____

_____

_____

_____

_____

Reflections

_____

_____

_____

_____

_____

_____

_____

_____

_____

_____

_____

_____

_____

_____

_____

_____

_____

_____

_____

_____

_____

_____

_____

_____

Now that you have learned the 10 principles of inner beauty transformation, it is my hope that you will keep these commandments near your heart and in your mind as you continue to give yourself the love and grace to evolve into the most beautiful version of yourself. This process is not a sprint to the finish line, but rather a marathon of continued living, learning and growing. Continue to journal, pray, meditate and prioritize your self-care, self-discovery and self-love.

With all my love,

Dr. Kym Lee King

Kym's Daily Affirmations
*MIND * BODY * SOUL*

Here is a list of biblical affirmations about our identity in Jesus Christ that is derived from a few selected passages in the New Testament. Whenever you forget WHO you are and how important you are reference these for strength. This is just a portion of the many truths about who we have become through faith in God's Son, but it is a powerful inventory to review from time to time. Hold these promises close to your heart, and read them daily until they saturate your mind.

1. **God loves me and has chosen me.**

   . . . knowing, brethren beloved by God, His choice of you. (1 Thessalonians 1:4)

2. **In Christ Jesus, I have wisdom, righteousness, sanctification, and redemption.**

   But by His doing you are in Christ Jesus, who became to us wisdom from God, and righteousness and sanctification, and redemption. (1 Corinthians 1:30)

3. **My body is a temple of the Holy Spirit who dwells in me.**

   Do you not know that you are a temple of God and that the Spirit of God dwells in you? . . . Or do you not know that your body is a temple of the Holy Spirit who is in you, whom you have from God, and that you are not your own? (1 Corinthians 3:16; 6:19)

4. **I am joined to the Lord and am one spirit with Him.**

   But the one who joins himself to the Lord is one spirit with Him. (1 Corinthians 6:17)

5. **God leads me in the triumph and knowledge of Christ.**

   But thanks be to God, who always leads us in triumph in Christ, and manifests through us the sweet aroma of the knowledge of Him in every place. (2 Corinthians 2:14)

6. **The hardening of my mind has been removed in Christ.**

   But their minds were hardened; for until this very day at the reading of the old covenant the same veil remains unlifted, because it is removed in Christ. (2 Corinthians 3:14)

7. **I am a new creature in Christ.**

    Therefore if anyone is in Christ, he is a new creature; the old things passed away; behold, new things have come. (2 Corinthians 5:17)

I have become the righteousness of God in Christ.

    He made Him who knew no sin to be sin on our behalf, so that we might become the righteousness of God in Him. (2 Corinthians 5:21)

8. **I have been made one with all who are in Christ Jesus.**

    There is neither Jew nor Greek, there is neither slave nor free man, there is neither male nor female; for you are all one in Christ Jesus. (Galatians 3:28)

9. **I am no longer a slave, but a child and an heir.**

    Therefore you are no longer a slave, but a son; and if a son, then an heir through God. (Galatians 4:7)

10. **I have been set free in Christ.**

    It was for freedom that Christ set us free; therefore keep standing firm and do not be subject again to a yoke of slavery. (Galatians 5:1)

11. **I have been blessed with every spiritual blessing in the heavenly places.**

    Blessed be the God and Father of our Lord Jesus Christ, who has blessed us with every spiritual blessing in the heavenly places in Christ. (Ephesians 1:3)

12. **I am chosen, holy, and blameless before God.**

    . . . just as He chose us in Him before the foundation of the world, that we would be holy and blameless before Him. (Ephesians 1:4)

13. **I am redeemed and forgiven by the grace of Christ.**

    In Him we have redemption through His blood, the forgiveness of our trespasses, according to the riches of His grace. (Ephesians 1:7)

14. **I have been predestined by God to obtain an inheritance.**

    In Him also we have obtained an inheritance, having been predestined according to His purpose who works all things after the counsel of His will. (Ephesians 1:10b–11)

15. **I have been sealed with the Holy Spirit of promise.**

    In Him, you also, after listening to the message of truth, the gospel of your salvation—having also believed, you were sealed in Him with the Holy Spirit of promise. (Ephesians 1:13)

16. **Because of God's mercy and love, I have been made alive with Christ.**

    But God, being rich in mercy, because of His great love with which He loved us, even when we were dead in our transgressions, made us alive together with Christ (by grace you have been saved). (Ephesians 2:4-5)

17. **I am seated in the heavenly places with Christ.**

    . . . and raised us up with Him, and seated us with Him in the heavenly places in Christ Jesus. (Ephesians 2:6)

18. **I am God's workmanship created to produce good works.**

    For we are His workmanship, created in Christ Jesus for good works, which God prepared beforehand so that we would walk in them. (Ephesians 2:10)

19. **I have been brought near to God by the blood of Christ.**

   But now in Christ Jesus you who formerly were far off have been brought near by the blood of Christ. (Ephesians 2:13)

20. **I am a member of Christ's body and a partaker of His promise.**

   . . . the Gentiles are fellow heirs and fellow members of the body, and fellow partakers of the promise in Christ Jesus through the gospel. (Ephesians 3:6; see also 5:30)

21. **I have boldness and confident access to God through faith in Christ.**

   . . . in whom we have boldness and confident access through faith in Him. (Ephesians 3:12)

22. **My new self is righteous and holy.**

   . . . put on the new self, which in the likeness of God has been created in righteousness and holiness of the truth. (Ephesians 4:24)

23. **I was formerly darkness, but now I am light in the Lord.**

   . . . you were formerly darkness, but now you are Light in the Lord; walk as children of Light. (Ephesians 5:8)

24. **I am a citizen of heaven.**

   For our citizenship is in heaven, from which also we eagerly wait for a Savior, the Lord Jesus Christ. (Philippians 3:20)

25. **The peace of God guards my heart and mind.**

   And the peace of God, which surpasses all comprehension, will guard your hearts and your minds in Christ Jesus. (Philippians 4:7)

God supplies all my needs.

Made in the USA
Columbia, SC
15 March 2020